Big Agile Roadmap:
Big Picture and Big Change

Ernest L. Hughes, Ed.D.

DEDICATION

This book is dedicated to the volunteers, professionals and social entrepreneurs who work to improve the quality of life of all those affected by hunger, homelessness, and mental ill-health through advocacy, education, and support. In the spirit of Conscious Capitalism®, the profits from the sale of this book will be donated to projects and organizations that support this mission.

CONTENTS

ACKNOWLEDGMENTS

CHANGE PLUS™ is a trademark of HughesGlobal, LLC.

Conscious Capitalism® is a registered trademark of Conscious Capitalism, Inc.

The Agile Fluency Model is copyright © 2012 by James Shore & Diana Larson. Used with permission.

The Manifesto for Agile Software Development - Agile Values, and Agile Principles are copyright © 2001 by the Agile Alliance. Used with permission.

1 INTRODUCTION

This book explores a hypothetical Big Agile Roadmap for increasing the adoption and scaling the practice of agile software development (ASD) across the enterprise in order to accelerate the creation, capture, and retention of value for an organization's stakeholders. Strategies for negotiating the right path and working together to effect change are discussed. Applied research, case studies, and emerging trends in ASD, Big Agile and Big Change are also examined. These findings are the result of ongoing applied research programs on Big Agile and Big Change, and two recent workshops on becoming a more agile organization.

The book contains nine chapters. Chapter 2 is a brief overview of the CHANGE PLUS™ service utilized to produce the roadmap. Chapter 3 contains and explains the Big Agile Roadmap. Chapter 4 outlines strategies for the right path, and Chapter 5 summarizes the research, studies and trends. Three learning aids are presented in Chapters 6 through 8 – a Knowledge Check, a Retrospective form, and a table of Useful Definitions.

The book concludes with a select list of useful articles and books in Chapter 9, and a list of useful web resources in Chapter 10. Some of these are referenced by number throughout the book as ① or ❶ respectively.

2 CHANGE PLUS™

The Big Agile Roadmap was created using the CHANGE PLUS™ service offered by HughesGlobal, LLC. This service creates change roadmaps utilizing a variety of development, design, evaluation, and change processes and recipes resulting in five plans:

1. Case for Change,
2. Communication,
3. Learning,
4. Transition, and
5. Sustainability.

Change Agents facilitate dialogue and conversation via action learning and collaborative coaching to develop these plans.

3 BIG AGILE ROADMAP

This chapter describes and presents a hypothetical Big Agile Roadmap for increasing the adoption and scaling the practice of agile software development (ASD) across the enterprise in order to accelerate the creation, capture, and retention of value for an organization's stakeholders.

Throughout this book, the word and concept *Agile* will generally mean a category of software development methodologies, and the word and concept *Agility* means a continual readiness to change.

Value can be defined and created in many different ways.

Value can be created through internal improvements or the exchange of ideas, knowledge, products, and services. ①

From a customer perspective, value is created from customer understanding and insight, and the application of the six principles of lean consumption like, "Don't make me wait." ⑦

From a strategic perspective, value can be created when learning is connected to strategy. Agility is a differentiator. ②

From a financial perspective, value is created when funds and resources are invested in the most profitable projects.

From a process perspective, value is created from knowledge flows across trusted networks such as COINs – Collaborative Innovation Networks. Product Development, Software Development, Quality & Continuous Improvement, Organizational Excellence, Enterprise Change Management,

Supply Chain Management, Innovation & Entrepreneurship are examples of such flows. ❹

The Big Agile Roadmap portrays a high-level conceptual model of these value creation approaches (Figure I).

As an organization seeks to expand and scale Agile Software Development (ASD), it will need to decide agility is a competitive differentiator, and create learning and value management structures such an Agile Working Group (AWG), Communities of Practice (COPs), and Enterprise Change Management.

Regular Curiosity, Clarity, and Values conversations, facilitated by Change Agents, are needed to overcome individual, organizational, and cultural resistance to change.

Increased value results when Agile practices move within and across teams and functional departments, then beyond organizational boundaries into supply chains and innovation networks.

Leadership agility is required to make these transitions happen.

Dr. J. Juran reminds us of the importance of overcoming organizational and cultural resistance to change.

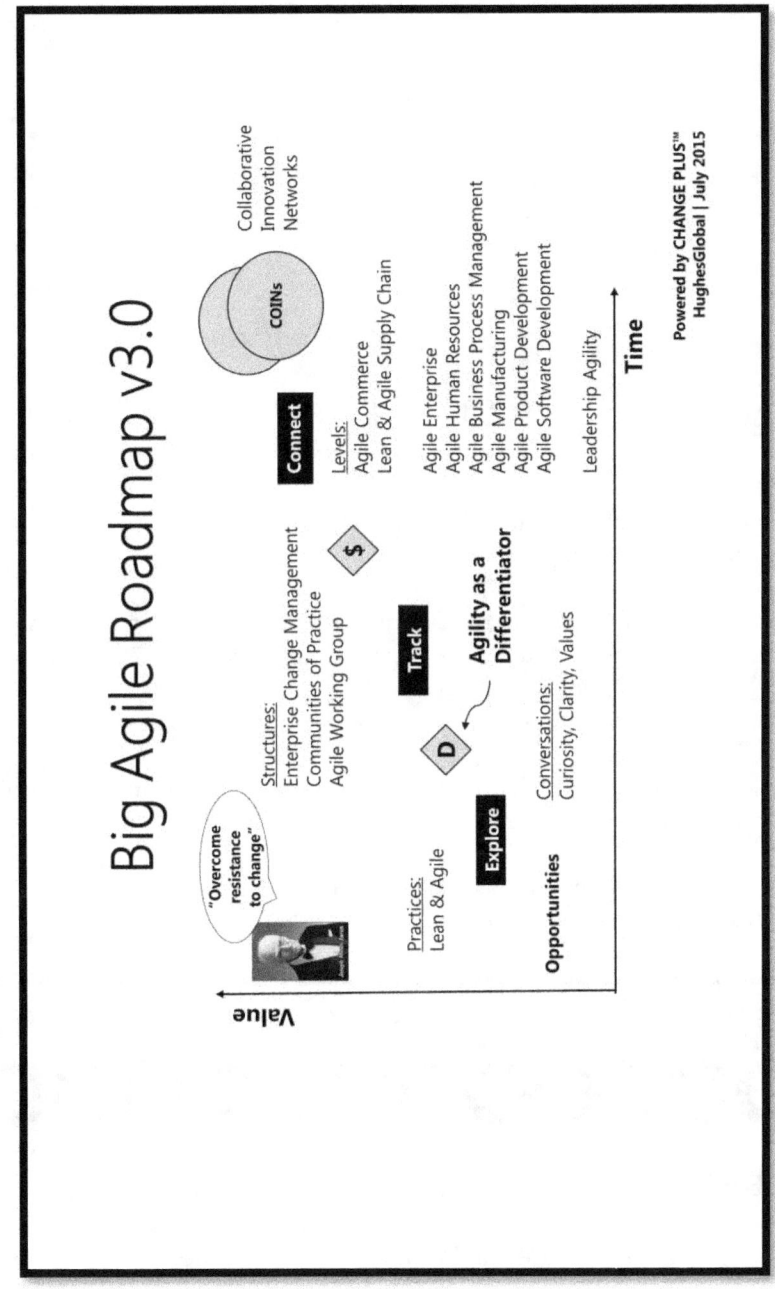

Figure 1. Big Agile Roadmap

4 STRATEGIES

Strategies for negotiating the right path an working together to effect change are discussed in this chapter.

Innovations in agile software development, agile product development, and agile manufacturing have unfolded separately and slowly over the past fifty years. The seminal paper on the classic "Waterfall model" for large software systems development was published in 1970. ⑤

The Harvard Business Review published a definitive paper on Agile Product Development in 1986. ⑥

Agile Manufacturing practices emerged in the 1990s. The Agile Manifesto for Software Development was published in 2001.

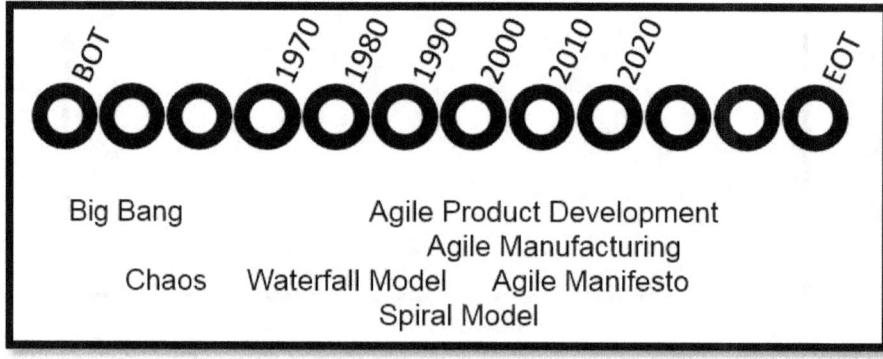

Figure 2. Agile Timeline

The Agile Fluency Model (Figure 3), published in 2012, portrays the Big Changes in team and organizational culture, skills and structures required to scale agility and increase value creation as highlighted in the Big Agile Roadmap.

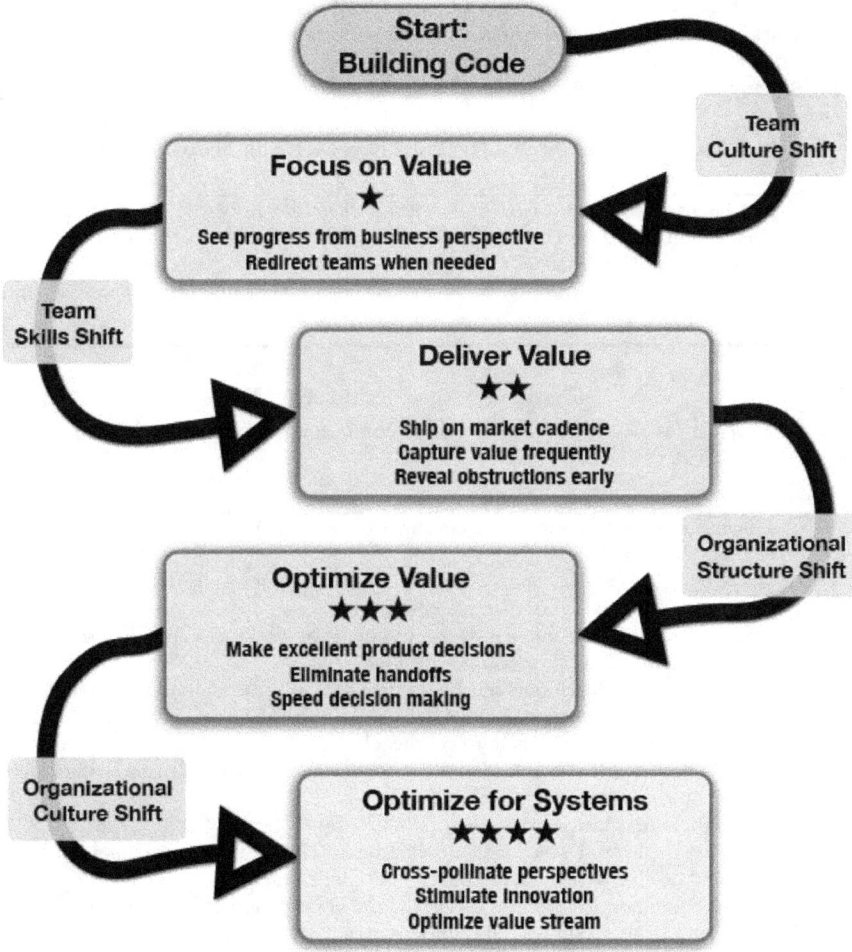

Figure 3. Agile Fluency Model ❷
Copyright © 2012. James Shore & Diana Larsen. Used with permission.

The values and value creation practices outlined in the Manifesto for Agile

Software Development (Figure 4), and the Agile Principles (Figure 5) are important inputs for the Curiosity, Clarification, and Values Conversations highlighted in the Big Agile Roadmap.

The Manifesto for Agile Software Development

We are uncovering better ways of developing software by doing it and helping other do it. Through this work we have come to value:

1. **Individuals and interactions** over processes and tools
2. **Working software** over comprehensive documentation
3. **Customer collaboration** over contract negotiation
4. **Responding to change** over following a plan

That is, while there is value in the items on the right, we value the items on the left more.

Kent Beck • James Grenning • Mike Beedle • Jim Highsmith • Robert C. Martin • Arie van Bennekum • Andrew Hunt • Steve Mellor • Alistair Cockburn • Ron Jeffries • Ken Schwaber • Ward Cunningham • Jon Kern • Jeff Sutherland • Martin Fowler • Brian Marick

Figure 4. Agile Values ❶
Copyright © 2001. Agile Alliance. Used with permission.

1.	Our highest priority is to satisfy the customer through early and continuous delivery of valuable software.
2.	Welcome changing requirements, even late in development. Agile processes harness change for the customer's competitive advantage.
3.	Deliver working software frequently, from a couple of weeks to a couple of months, with a preference for the shorter timescale.
4.	Business people and developers must work together daily throughout the project.
5.	Build projects around motivated individuals. Give them the environment and support they need, and trust them to get the job done.
6.	The most efficient and effective method of conveying information to and within a development team is face-to-face conversation.
7.	Working software is the primary measure of progress.
8.	Agile processes promote sustainable development. The sponsors, developers, and users should be able to maintain a constant pace indefinitely.
9.	Continuous attention to technical excellence and good design enhances agility.
10.	Simplicity-the art of maximizing the amount of work not done-is essential.
11.	The best architectures, requirements, and designs emerge from self-organizing teams.
12.	At regular intervals, the team reflects on how to become more effective, then tunes and adjusts its behavior accordingly.

Figure 5. Agile Principles ❶
Copyright © 2001. Agile Alliance. Used with permission.

Motivation for organizational adoption of agile software development practices include better software quality, higher productivity, improved predictability, and increased customer satisfaction.

Motivation for adoption of agile software development practices by developers include pride in ownership, craftsmanship, the team, and choice autonomy – the ability to direct choices in order to be effective.

The importance of intrinsic motivation cannot be overstated. In 2012, I visited the Philadelphia Museum of Art while attending a seminar. I watched a sedan pull up along the curb while standing on the street near the famous statue featured in the movie Rocky. Four men in suits, ties, and dress shoes hopped out, and sprinted up the 72 "Rocky steps." ❾ They raised their arms in victory at the top, then skipped back down to the car and drove off. Many others have been motivated to do so.

It can be challenging for individuals and teams to stay motivated when practicing agile in a mostly non-agile world. From a systems perspective, you cannot be what the larger system is not, at least for very long.

Managing change is required for adopting and practicing ASD. Agile aspiration statements (Value #4, Principle #12) provide guidance for addressing change incrementally.

Expanding and scaling ASD across an organization requires Big Change.

Almost all approaches to Big Change rest or draw upon Lewin's three-stage Change Model – Unfreezing → Moving → Freezing, or his Force Field Analysis (of Feasibility) – Forces For versus Forces Against Change.

Figure 6 depicts the Change Model, and Figure 7 is an illustrative template for performing Force Field Analysis.

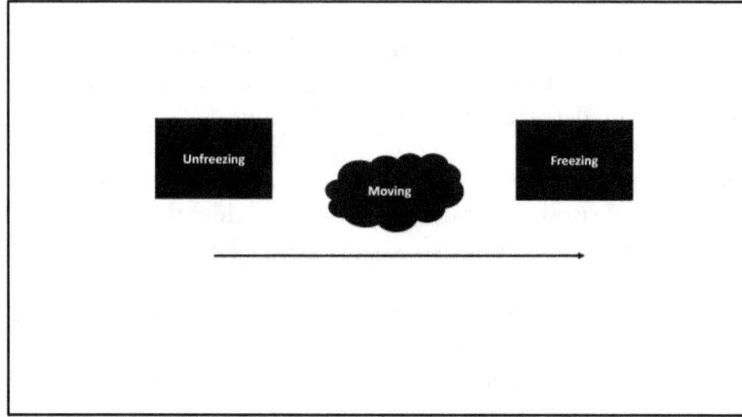

Figure 6. Lewin's Change Model

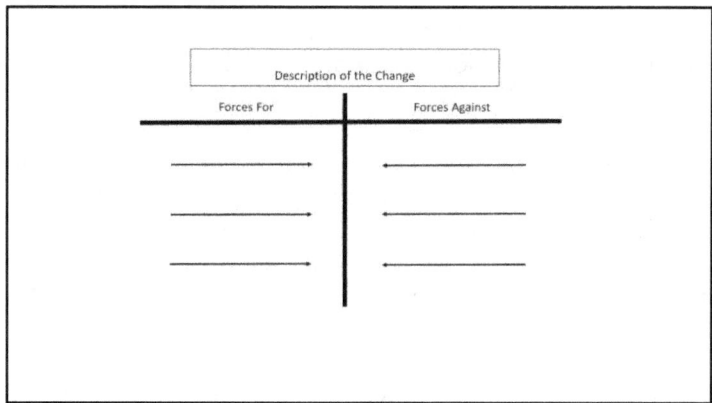

Figure 7. Lewin's Force Field Analysis (of Feasibility)

These models assume that motivation for change must be generated before change can occur. Some organizations experience so much compound change that they never refreeze, existing in a sort of permanent permafrost state.

Many times, Change Agents try to increase the for forces for change when they perceive resistance is increasing. A better strategy is to try to relax one or more of the forces against.

Inherent in both Small and Big Change is determining the proportion of activities related to preparation versus implementation. In other words,

"How much planning do you do?"

Motivation, development, and "change-ability" for individuals and teams can also be looked at from a strengths perspective. According to the Strength Finders 2.0 assessment, my top five strengths are: Learner, Relator, Futuristic, Strategic, and Achiever. ❿

Agile methods accommodate change differently.

In Scrum-based Development, changes are not allowed once a sprint has started. Extreme Programming (XP) changes are accepted in later stages. Kanban allows change at any time. ④

5 RESEARCH & TRENDS

Applied research, case studies, and emerging trends in ASD, Big Agile and Big Change are examined in this chapter.

Here are some notable findings from research on the application of ASD:

1. Agile methods are not typically used completely. There is a higher adoption of Scrum over XP and Lean.

2. Daily Scrums can be less frequent, and of longer duration.

3. Planning poker is the most common method of effort estimation. Typically, effort is underestimated.

4. To improve your ability to overcome Impediments, diagram them and assess your ability to influence resolution.

5. Personality may determine a preference for Agile.

6. Scrum Masters may be overloaded with the number challenging roles they perform.

7. According to studies presented at the 2013 Scrum PLoP Conference, 42% of Agile projects are successful, 49% are late or over budget, and 9% are total failures. Additionally, teams that finish early do so by accelerating faster.

Here are some notable results from case studies of the application of ASD:

1. Agile Portfolio Management, utilizing a Kanban portfolio, increased project throughput by 20%.

2. Ericsson Telecom utilized a lean philosophy, Agile mindset, and organizational change management for a large-scale system transformation – over 2000 employees across 10 global locations with a code base of approximately 40 million lines.

3. An enterprise roll out of Agile successfully launched 30 teams simultaneously, utilizing a "Coach of Coaches" approach.

4. Scrum was utilized on a high stakes project by an organization seeking to renew its Agile effort beyond a stalled XP pilot.

5. A large-scale agile change effort by the HP FutureSmart Firmware team supporting a 20-year legacy of Laserjet software resulted in an eight week delivery cycle while reducing development costs 40%.

6. A multi-site, multi-product organization with integrated product management utilized virtual Scrum Teams to deliver releases in 1/3 the time.

7. A University IT department utilized Agile to reduce deliver time by 50%, and created happy teams doing so.

Here are some emerging trends on the application of ASD:

1. Forrester reports that many organizations are utilizing a hybrid combination of Waterfall and Agile approaches, sometimes referred to as Water-Scrum-fall.

2. Martin Fowler recently called for the need for an agile (little "a") orthodox revival.

3. The Agile Alliance noted alignment efforts with other disciplines. Examples: Agile Project Management and Agile Accounting. ❶

4. PuppetLabs highlighted the increasing integration of Development and Operations (DevOps). Netflix's *NoOps* is an case in point.

5. In his most recent book, Dr. John Kotter emphasizes the need for accelerating change. ❿

6. A Georgia Tech Study found that both speed and quality are expected today.

7. Similarly, Gartner reports that Big Change is required to achieve efficiency and growth simultaneously.

8. Wegner-Trayner's Social Learning Framework can be utilized to move beyond Seinfeld Learning ("No learning, no hugging"). ❽

Even though Agile is fifteen years old, advances in Agile principles and practices are continuing to be made. CoPs like BeyondAgile and the Agile Alliance are good sources to keep up to date on research, emerging trends, and experiences. ❸ ❶

6 KNOWLEDGE CHECK

Here is a list of important concepts to remember.

- ✓ Value is co-created with customers.
- ✓ The system cannot work unless you understand the system.
- ✓ You cannot be what the larger system is not (at least for very long).
- ✓ Build on strengths.
- ✓ Knowledge flows across trusted networks (COINs & CoPs).

7 RETROSPECTIVE

Use this form to define goals for your agile journey. Consider individual, team, organization, and value chain levels. What are you going to do more of (+)? What are your going to do less of (-)? Share with your networks (COINS & CoPs).

+	-

8 USEFUL DEFINITIONS

Here is a list of useful definitions.

Term / Concept	Definition
Agile	Category of software development methodologies
Agility	Continual readiness to change
ASD	Agile Software Development
AWG	Agile Working Group
BDD	Behavioral Driven Development (Variant of TDD)
BVC	Big Visible Chart
COINs	Collaborative Innovation Networks
CoPs	Communities of Practice
DevOps	Development and Operations
DoD	Definition of Done; "done – done"
ECM	Enterprise Change Management
Green Tomato	Potential to develop lies ahead
Impediment	Anything that obstructs the smooth flow of work
Innovation	Useful improvements in existing technologies, ideas, processes, products, or services
Leagile	Lean and Agile
LSD	Lean Software Development
Shift Left	Operations concerns move closer to Development
TDD	Test-Driven Development
XP	eXtreme Programming
YAGNI	You Aren't Going to Need It

9 RESOURCES

Here is a select list of useful resources.

(1) Demirkan, H., Spohrer, J., & Krishna, V. (Eds.). (2011). *Service systems implementation.* New York: Springer.

(2) Hambrick, D., & Fredrickson, J. (2001, Nov.). Are you sure you have a strategy? *The Academy of Management Executive*, 15(4), 48-59.

(3) Kotter, J. (2014) *Accelerate: Building strategic agility for a faster-moving world.* Cambridge, MA: Harvard Business Review Press.

(4) Matharu, G., Mishra, A., Singh, H., & Upadhyay, P. (2015, January). Empirical study of agile software development methodologies: A comparative analysis. *ACM SIGSOFT Software Engineering Notes*, 40(1), 1-5.

(5) Royce, W. (1970, August). Managing the development of large software systems. *IEEE WESCON*, pp 1-9.

(6) Takeuchi, H. & Nonaka, I. (1986). The new new product development game. *Harvard Business Review.*

(7) Womack, J. & Jones, D. (2005, March). Lean consumption. *Harvard Business Review.*

10 WEB RESOURCES

Here is a select list of useful web resources.

1 Agile Alliance, http://www.agilealliance.org

2 Agile Fluency, http://www.agilefluency.com

3 Beyond Agile, http://www.beyondagile.org

4 Enterprise Change Management,
http://www.prosci.com/ecm1/overview/

5 Jama, http://www.jamasoftware.com/

6 Leankit Kanban System, http://leankit.com/kanban/kanban-system/

7 Ideascale, http://ideascale.com/

8 Social Learning video [2:15m – 4:33m],
https://youtu.be/qvighN3BDmI

9 Rocky Steps, http://en.wikipedia.org/wiki/Rocky_Steps

10 StrengthsFinder Assessment,
https://www.gallupstrengthscenter.com/Purchase/en-US/Index

ABOUT THE AUTHOR

Ernest L. Hughes ("Ernie" or "Lincoln") is a Senior Management Consultant, Business Coach, and Managing Partner of HughesGlobal, LLC, his consulting and education network focused on helping individuals, teams, organizations, and value chains realize their potential and flourish through leadership development and organizational learning. He is also an Associate Professor in the School of Business for American Public University System, an Adjunct Professor in Information Systems Management at Seattle Pacific University, and a part-time Lecturer for Executive Education for the University of Washington Bothell.

Prior to launching is consulting and education network, Hughes enjoyed broad leadership responsibility in a range of organizations for more than thirty years. He was most recently Director of Technical Services for Recreational Equipment, Inc. Before joining REI, Hughes was co-founder, Chief Information Officer and Director of Information & Learning Systems & Technology for Cascadia College after a fifteen-year technology career with Boeing. At Boeing, he managed business applications, systems engineering, application architecture, software process improvement, software cost management, software engineering education, and merger integration functions and programs. He started his career as a software developer.

Hughes earned a Master of Science degree in Global Supply Chain Management from the University of Alaska Anchorage, A Doctorate in Educational Leadership and a Masters in Software Engineering from Seattle University, a MBA from the California State University, Bakersfield, an a Bachelor of Science degree in Computer Science from California Polytechnic University, San Luis Obispo. He has training and certification in a number of specialties, including management of quality / organizational excellence from ASQ, and change management from Prosci.

www.ingramcontent.com/pod-product-compliance
Lightning Source LLC
Chambersburg PA
CBHW070927180526
45168CB00005B/2185